*Original choral verses
for the primary and
intermediate grades
by RITA BRYAN*

Choral Speaking

Lear Siegler, Inc./Fearon Publishers
Belmont, California

*Designed and illustrated
by Jane Mitchell.*

ISBN-0-8224-1359-0.

Library of Congress Catalog Card Number: 73-77483.

Printed in the United States of America.

Contents

Many elementary school teachers have used choral
reading in their classes. But choral *speaking* differs from
choral reading in that the children do not read from a book
—they memorize a passage of poetry or prose and then
speak as a group. Memorization is easy for children, and it
frees them to use their hands and arms for expressive
gestures.

It is important to give your class the proper start in
choral speaking. Explain to them that they will be a choir
that speaks instead of a choir that sings. They have all
heard choirs, either in church or on television. Remind them
that sometimes a choir sings as a unit, and, at times, a solo,
a duet, a trio, or a quartet contributes to the presentation.
A speaking choir works the same way.

Have the children choose a nursery rhyme (primary
grades) or a favorite short poem they all know (intermediate
grades). Say the poem to them *slowly and with expression*.
Then have the class say it at the same speed. You might
let the girls say a couple of lines, the boys a couple of lines,
or ask one child to try a solo line.

Then read the class a poem from this book, *slowly and
with expression*. If you do not start out this way, it will be
difficult to halt their speedy, sing-song method of recitation.
I'd suggest that you follow these steps:

1. Ask the children to repeat the poem after you, line for
   line, just as you want them to say it.
2. Alternate between the boys and the girls, so repetition
   will not become monotonous.

3. Have the children copy the poem as a writing lesson, or have them make a choral speaking book to use all year.
4. Ask everyone to have the poem memorized by a designated date.
5. When they all know the poem, assign the solo parts as suggested to the left of the text. Seat the girls (or High V.) on one side of the room, and the boys (or Low V.) on the other side. Those chosen to speak special parts should sit in front or at the ends of rows. Go through the poem once or twice while the class is seated.
6. Now have the class stand at the front of the room in the same formation and say the poem again. Let the students suggest appropriate gestures. These should be made in unison by a small group or by the entire class.

At Levels A and B the teacher makes the best director. Your hands will let the children know what you expect of them. It doesn't take a class long to learn your cues for a group or a soloist to speak, or for changes in volume or speed. Later, students at Level C may want to choose a director from among themselves.

Choral speaking benefits the entire class. It is a group project that unites the students as few other projects do. If the class practices choral speaking every week, you will soon notice how shy children begin to forget their shyness, and how aggressive children learn to work with the group. Choral speaking is an activity that both you and the children will enjoy.

Rita Bryan

Level A

BACK TO SCHOOL

Chorus	It's good to come back to school
	When long summer days have passed;
Solo	I like to see all my friends
Chorus	And get down to work at last.

FALL SONG

Girls	Bright leaves falling,
Boys	Wild geese calling,
All	Can you guess the time of year?
Girls	Witches riding,
Boys	Goblins hiding,
All	Seem to say that fall is here.

ON THE PLAYGROUND

All Out on the playground
   We all like to play,
Girls And that's where we go
   Every suitable day.
Boys We learn to be careful,
   Avoid being rough;
Solo 1 We share all our playthings—
All There's always enough.
Solo 2 We must take our turn
   On the slides and the swings,
Girls And when we have finished
   We put away things.
Boys Yes, out on the playground
   We all like to play,
All So we hope that it's always
   A suitable day.

CROSSING THE STREET

Girls Whenever I want to cross the street,
Boys I look each way with care,
All Then walk quite straight and quickly
   Till I find that I am there.

BOOTS

All	"Swish, swoosh," go my boots
	On the dewy ground,
Girls	Forming little droplets
	That fly around and 'round.
All	"Slip, slop," go my boots
	In the puddle brown,
Boys	Getting me all dirty
	As I slosh them up and down.
All	"Crinch, crunch," go my boots
	On the solid snow,
Girls	Making marching music
	No matter where I go.
Boys	"Come, come, happy child,"
Girls	My lovely boots will say;
All	"In any kind of weather
	You and I can run and play."

LEARNING DOUBLES

Chorus	6 and 6 are 12
	And 2 and 2 are 4 ;
Girls	I'm learning all my doubles
	So let me tell you more.
Boys	4 and 4 are 8
	And 1 and 1 are 2,
Quartet	5 and 5 are 10 ;
	Those are easy ones to do.
Girls	7 and 7 are 14,
	3 and 3 are 6 ;
Boys	If I don't learn the others
	I'll be in quite a fix.
Quartet	9 and 9 are 18,
Girls	10 and 10 are 20,
Boys	8 and 8 are 16 ;
Chorus	For little folks that's plenty !

PRETTY TOES

All	Ten pretty little toes
	On two pretty little feet ;
Girls	Mother pulls them gently
	And sings a song so sweet,
Boys	About "Piggie goes to market,
	Stays home another time,"
All	And Baby laughs and gurgles
	At the funny little rhyme.

TWINS

Chorus	I know some twins named Mary and Ro;
	They're always together wherever they go.
High V.	When one sighs, the other sighs;
Low V.	When one cries, the other cries.
Solo	And when it's rainy weather,
Chorus	They both get colds together.
Quartet	They have such fun when out at play,
	They're never lonesome any day.
Chorus	I wonder what it's like to be
	A twin to someone just like me!

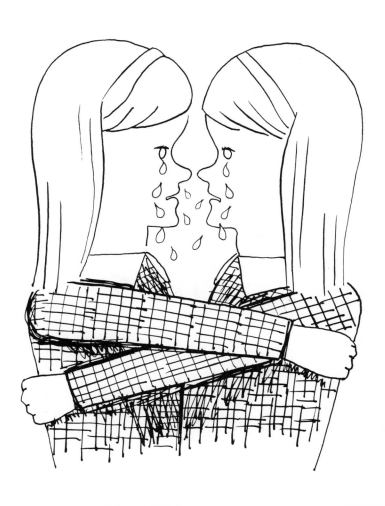

FIREMEN

Boys	Every time I hear a siren
	Shriek and wail and bawl,
All	I think about the firemen
	Who answer every call.
Girls	They must risk their lives for people,
	Try to stop the fire;
Quartet	Bravery they do possess
All	And this we all admire.

FIRE PREVENTION WEEK

Quartet	Since this is Fire Prevention Week,
	Your best attention we now seek
Chorus	So we can help you, when you play,
	To keep fire accidents away.
Solo 1	Matches you must use with care;
Chorus	We don't want our trees all bare!
Solo 2	Don't touch electric plugs and wires
Chorus	And then we'll all be safe from fires.

THE POLICEMAN

All   I have a friend who means a lot
To all my family;
Girls   He walks around our neighborhood
And watches out for me.
Boys   This is a fine policeman
Who tries to battle crime;
All   He wants to be a faithful friend
And help us all the time.

MY DENTIST

All   I go to see my dentist
Every chance I get;
He's always been so nice to me
Ever since we met.
Solo 1   He shows me how the chair works,
Solo 2   Explains to me the drill;
Solo 3   I love to go to see him—
All   I'm sure I always will.

HALLOWEEN PARTY

All   We have such fun on Halloween
In our classroom here at school;

Girls   We put on costumes after lunch
For a party, as a rule.

Boys   Our teacher goes outside the door,
Then we put masks on too;

All   When someone tells her to come back,
She's scared as we yell, "BOO!"

Girls   Then after songs and jokes and all
Solo   We end the day by eating,
Boys   So we're all set, when we reach home,
To start our trick or treating.

CHRISTMAS LIST

All   What do I want for Christmas?
I don't want much, you know—
Girls   Just one small stove like Mother's,
Boys   A table, nice and low,
Girls   A tea set made of plastic,
Boys   Some blocks that I can build,
All   And when I hang my stocking,
I hope it will be filled!
Girls   Oh yes, I want a dolly
Just like a real live bride,
Boys   Perhaps a shiny new bike
So I could take a ride.
Girls   A velvet dress with sequins
Would make me look so sweet,
All   And how about a puppy dog?
I'd walk him on the street.
Boys   And maybe, too, a midget car
With tires, brake, and clutch,
All   And then perhaps—but do you think
I'm asking for too much?

JACK FROST

All   Jack Frost paints icy pictures
Upon my windowpane,
Solo   But I just take a little cloth
All   And wipe them off again.

RIDE ON A JET

All	I'd sure like to bet
	That a ride on a jet
	Would be pretty exciting and thrilling.
Boys	We'd zoom through the air
	Without worry or care,
	Just as fast as the pilot was willing.
Girls	As we zipped through the sky
	The clouds would pass by;
	All of the ride would be pleasant.
Boys	I'd make Mom understand,
	And Dad, too, when we land,
All	That I'd like a jet for a present.

RIDDLES

All	"I'll tell you a riddle," said Jock.
	"It's what can be found in a sock.
Boys	The length of a ruler,
	A part of your bed,
Girls	A big hint I'll give you—
	It's *not* the head!
Boys	It rhymes with 'put';
	What is it?"
All	FOOT
All	"I'll tell you another," said Si.
	It sometimes is found in a pie.
Trio 1	With only one pit,
	It's small, red, and round,
Trio 2	It grows on the tree
	That George chopped to the ground.
Boys	It rhymes with 'ferry';
	What is it?"
All	CHERRY

Girls "I have a good riddle," said Mae.
    "We use it not only for play.
Duet 1 We can ride it to school
    Instead of the bus,
Duet 2 Or to shop at the store
    When Mother asks us.
Girls It rhymes with 'hike';
    What is it?"
All BIKE

Girl Trio "I have a good one," said Sue.
    "It's something familiar to you.
Girls I can rest in the park
    On one long and wide;
Boy Trio Our big picnic table
    Has one at each side.
Boys It rhymes with 'wrench';
    What is it?"
All BENCH

Boys "I have a hard one," said Lou.
    "It sometimes is found in a zoo.
Girls With fangs, without feet,
    It slithers about,
All But if it is poison,
    We have to watch out!
Boys It rhymes with 'lake';
    What is it?"
All SNAKE

All "Now I have one more," said Dee.
    "It's something so lovely to see.
Girls It's soft, white, and cold
    When starting to fall;
Boys When there is enough,
    We can make *man* or *ball*.
Girls It rhymes with 'throw';
    What is it?"
All SNOW

DREAMS

Girls	Sometimes at night when I'm asleep I dream a dream or two.
Solo	I've had some really lovely ones,
All	I've had some bad ones too.
Boys	The bad ones seem all dark and dim And scare me, I must say;
Girls	The good ones are a fluffy ball, All bouncy, light, and gay.
Duet	I hope tonight when I'm asleep My dreams are good, 'cause then
All	I'm sure to wake up with a smile When morning comes again.

CINDY

Solo 1	Cindy's hair is red—
All	She's a real cute curlyhead.
Girls	She loves to dance and sing, As she makes her red curls swing.
Boys	I said, "What will you be When you grow up big like me?"
Solo 2	Can you guess at Cindy's answer?
All	"A red-haired, singing dancer!"

MAGIC *(Girls)*

All   I went to the hairdresser's yesterday;
Trio   He put me up in a chair
      And started fixing, bit by bit,
      My straight and stubborn hair.
Solo   But later on, in wonderment,
      I asked him, "Can it be?"
All   For looking from the mirror
      Was a curly beauty—ME!

BOOK FRIENDS

All	When you're thinking of good friends,
Boys	Do you include good books?
Girls	Don't they all look handsome
	On their shelves or in their nooks?
Solo 1	Be gentle with these book-friends;
Solo 2	Repair them now and then,
All	So you will have them many years
	To read and read again.

LINCOLN'S STORIES

Solo	Lincoln was a storyteller;
	He gathered round him folks
All	Who liked to listen to his tales
	And good amusing jokes.
Boys	In spite of all his busyness,
	He made these people smile;
Girls	It does us good to stop our work
All	And laugh once in a while.

SALUTE TO WASHINGTON

Girls When Washington was president,
Our country was so new
Boys That he was first of all of them
All And praise to him is due.
Boys Our country's well-known capital
Girls Was named for him, you know;
All So let's salute George Washington
Who helped our country grow.

WASHINGTON'S TRUTHFULNESS

Chorus Washington never told a lie
And, though he knew he'd catch it,
Low V. He said, "*I* chopped the cherry tree—
I did it with my hatchet!"
High V. His father was quite angry
But a spanking he passed by,
Because his son was truthful;
All George hadn't told a lie.

THANK YOU

Boys When you've been given something new,
Girls Or someone has been kind to you,
Trio By helping you in some small way,
All Say, "Thank you"—you'll feel good all day.

PLAYING COWBOY *(Boys)*

Solo 1	I love to play cowboy outside in our yard;
Solo 2	I get all excited and play very hard,
Solo 3	Because I'm not really a boy having fun—
All	I'm really a cowboy with lasso and gun.
High V.	I make quite a business of rounding up herds
	With the help of my dog and a few cowboy words.
Low V.	Then at rodeo time I win prizes galore,
	For roping a calf and for doing lots more.
Solo 4	But after I've played for an hour or so,
Solo 5	My hunger commences to grow and to grow.
All	My arms are so tired, my feet feel like lead,
	And nothing's so good as my "little boy" bed.

MY BIKE

Chorus   I ride my red bike every day
               The weather will permit,
Duet   But I am careful on the road
               So I will not get hit.
Boys   I don't go in the parts of town
               Where traffic's never done;
Girls   I ride my bike on quiet streets—
Chorus   That's where I have my fun.

DOCTOR FRIEND

Solo 1   Sometimes I cannot go to school;
Solo 2   I have to stay in bed,
Chorus   Because I have a fever
               Or a bad cold in my head.
Girls   Then Mommy calls the doctor—
               He tells her I must rest
Boys   And orders medication
               That for me will be the best.
Solo 3   The next day I am better,
Solo 4   And now I feel just fine.
Chorus   That's why our family doctor
               Is a special friend of mine.

KITCHEN BAND

All	Did you ever play in a kitchen band?
Girls	You use things from the kitchen.
Boys	A breadboard makes a good wood block
All	When rhythm's got you itchin'!
Girls	A pie tin and an old cheap spoon,
Boys	A small washboard so snazzy,
All	All help to make a kitchen band
	Play music that is jazzy.

*(Use this poem with instruments.
Have children play a song or two.)*

MAKE-BELIEVE TRAIN

All	In school we make a big long train
	Of children 'stead of cars;
Boys	We chug and chug around the room,
	Our arms connecting bars.
Solo 1	Sometimes I am the engine,
Solo 2	Sometimes the red caboose,
Girls	Or else the man who tightens up
	The bars we've shaken loose.
Solo 3	We all become the whistle
Boys	As a loud "toot, toot" we shout,
All	Then guide the train to the roundhouse
	When we're all tired out.

MOTHERS

All   Mothers are a special kind
      Of people, as you know;
Boys They help us in so many ways
      To act right and to grow.
Girls But here's a little secret,
      Just in case you haven't guessed:
Solo Of all the mothers in the world,
All   *My* mother is the best.

IN SCHOOL

Girls Be quietly gay,
      Obey every rule,
Boys Each part of the day
      That you are in school.
All   Laugh and shout
      When school is out!

JUNE

Girls June is the month of roses,
Solo A wonderful, beautiful time.
Boys It makes everybody feel happy—
All   That's why I'm reciting this rhyme!

EASTER BUNNY

All   An Easter bunny's very cute;
Solo 1   He wriggles up his little snoot
Girls   And hops around as light as air,
    So that you wonder if he's there.
Boys   And even when he's just "pretend,"
Solo 2   A cotton tail stuck on his end,
All   He's loved by folks in every clime
    Because he's part of Easter time.

HEALTHY BOY

Boys   A healthy boy is a happy boy;
Solo   He's never cross or mean.
Girls   He looks at life with sparkling eyes—
All   To him everything is keen.

SCHOOL

All   School is a wonderful place to be,
Girls   The place where we learn to hear and see
Boys   A number of things that will make us wise,
All   If only we'll open our ears and eyes.

PLEASE

Girls	"Please" is such a little word,
Boys	It takes you just a minute.
Solo	But oh, it means so much to folks,
All	So put your heart right in it.

FATHERS

Boys	Fathers are strong and loving And helpful as they can be;
Girls	They never complain about working To buy things for you and me.
All	They teach us games and fishing, Protect us, every one;
Boys	We call them and they come running,
Girls	No matter what we've done.
All	We love them and they know it— Now let's begin to show it!

LITTLE BIRD

Boys	I saw a little bird hopping brightly along;
Girls	He pecked at the grass, then sang a merry song.
Solo 1	He seemed so happy I thought I'd say a word
All	Or perhaps two or three to the cute little bird.
Solo 2	As I walked quickly up to where he had stopped,
Girls	He noticed me coming, so away he hopped;
Boys	When I came too near, he glanced at me,
All	Spread out his pretty wings and flew up into a tree.

PAINTING

Girls   Finger painting's lots of fun,
  All   You swish and swirl until you're done.
Boys   We can paint with brushes too;
  All   I just love to paint, don't you?

RAIN IS GOOD

Boys   I really love to watch the rain
          As it drizzles to the ground,
  All   Or even when it pours down fast
          And makes a thund'rous sound.
Girls   For then I feel secure and safe;
          My family is near
 Trio   And we can always have some fun—
  All   The rain can't reach us here.
Boys   We make our own bright atmosphere,
Girls   An indoor kind of sun,
  All   For we have learned to love the rain
          And so can everyone.

IT'S OCTOBER

Girls   Why are the birds all flying from town?
          Why are the red and brown leaves falling
            down?
Boys   Why are the days getting chilly and clear?
  All   It's 'cause October is here.

MR. WIND

Trio   March is such a windy month,
We have to watch our step,
Chorus   For after all our winter colds,
We're pretty low in pep.
Low V.   Mr. Wind is blustery
And noisy as can be;
High V.   He sighs and moans and rattles things
Chorus   But he can't frighten *me*.
Low V.   I'll surely take my vitamins
High V.   And play outdoors at noon,
Chorus   For Mr. Wind is telling us
That spring will be here soon.

MY VALENTINE

Solo   Although I'm small, as you can see,
         (Mom)
On this my (Dad) and I agree:
    (Daddy)
My (Mommy) is my valentine;
       (his)   (he)
I know I'm (hers) 'cause (she) is mine.

(If a girl says it, she uses the top words.
If a boy says it, he uses the bottom words.)

MY DOG

All   My dog is a wonderful pup;
Boys   On his hind legs he stands right up.
Girls   He begs for his food
          When he feels in the mood—
All   He's a nice little, cute little pup.

TWO TOTS

Chorus   Two little tots were fighting,
           Both battering and biting.
High V.   "Tut, tut!" their mothers told them
           As they started in to scold them.
Low V.   The tots' clothes were in tatters,
           Not that that really matters;
Chorus   The point we want to stress
           Is that tots should fight much less.

JIMMY PATTE

Girls	Wee Jimmy Patte
	Had one old hat
	With such a funny feather;
Boys	As sure as fate
	It stood up straight
	In bright and sunny weather.
Trio	But when it rained
	And skies were stained
	With clouds all gray and brown,
All	The feather bright
	To Jim's delight
	Would turn quite upside down.

PARAKEETS

Chorus	Parakeets are pretty,
	Parakeets are gay,
Low V.	And I have one at my house
	Who talks to me all day.
High V.	His feathers look so lovely,
	His chirping sounds so sweet;
Chorus	Life wouldn't be the same for me
	Without my parakeet.

SCHOOL IS OVER

All	I'm glad that school is over
Girls	And my lessons are all done;
Boys	Now I'm going to pitch right in
All	And have a lot of fun.

POLITENESS

Girls	Be polite in every way
Boys	Every minute of the day.
Solo	If you go to visit, then
All	You'll be asked to come again.

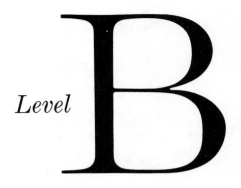

Level **B**

SEPTEMBER

Chorus	Summer's almost over
	And we've started back to school;
Girls	Days still seem like summer
Boys	Though September nights are cool.
Duet	Come, forget the summer;
Boys	We can do it if we try,
Girls	For there's promise of the autumn
Chorus	As September days pass by.

FOOLISH BOY

Boys	I know a boy named Buddy;
All	His last name's McGillicuddy.
Girls	He just goes to school
	To play and to fool—
All	It's plain that he hates to study.
All	BUT
Solo 1	Unless he can spell,
All	He won't turn out well.
Solo 2	If his English is poor,
All	He'll be labeled a boor.
Solo 3	And if he can't add,
All	Too bad, too bad!

LITTLE JOAN

Chorus	A very small girl with a very sore throat Was sent home from school with the following note:
High V.	"Your little girl Joan is quite sick, Mrs. Pratt, With something the doctor should really look at."
Low V.	They went to the doctor's that very same night, Hoping that he would make everything right.
Solo 1	The doctor examined her thoroughly, then—
Solo 2	He examined her over again.
Chorus	The advice that he gave was to soon have removed Her poor diseased tonsils, for useless they'd proved.
Low V.	So, in due course of time, Joan was scrubbed clean and dressed And all shared in hoping that she'd stand the test.
High V.	But she cried as she entered the hospital door And succeeded in hurting her throat even more.
Solo 3	Her mother and father were worried to death—
Chorus	Through the whole operation, they both held their breath.
Solo 4	The funniest part of this true little rhyme
Low V.	Is that once it was over she had the best time.
High V.	All the doctors and nurses were under her spell And she wanted to stay there she liked it so well!

CHRISTMAS TREE

Chorus   Gather near the Christmas tree,
           Sing a Christmas song;
Low V.   Hear the way our voices blend,
           Merrily and strong.
High V. What a happy family!
           Merry as can be!
Trio   Every present's neatly wrapped
           Underneath the tree.
Low V.   Christmas wouldn't seem so bright
High V. Nor home be quite so gay
Chorus   Without a lovely Christmas tree
           On merry Christmas Day.

OCTOBER

Duet 1	Put on your new dress, October,
	The one with the orange and brown,
Girls	And tie in your hair a ribbon of red
	To show off your beautiful gown.
Boys	Make all the leaves start falling
	In colorful heaps on the ground;
Duet 2	Some day, when you're feeling playful,
	Blow them and swirl them around.
Girls	Whisper to children, "Wear sweaters!"
Boys	Tell them that autumn is here.
Solo	Then fool them with warm days, October,
All	Most colorful month of the year.

COLUMBUS DAY

All	Columbus was courageous,
	His mind was clear and sound;
Girls	He wished to prove to people
	This earth of ours was round.
Boys	Columbus crossed the ocean
	Together with his crew,
All	And finally they reached here
	In fourteen ninety-two.
Solo 1	October twelfth the date was;
All	His crew sent up a cheer!
Solo 2	We call this day Columbus Day
All	And honor him each year.

MUSIC WEEK

All   National Music Week is here;
Boys   For this we give a rousing cheer,
Girls   Each man and woman, girl and boy,
All   Since music's what we all enjoy.

FIRE

All   How wonderful is fire
     When we use it as we should!
Boys   It heats our homes through oil or gas
     And sometimes firewood.
Girls   It cooks our food and keeps it
     As hot as we may wish;
Solo 1   We need it in the park to cook
     Our favorite picnic dish.
All   How terrible is fire
     When it's gotten out of hand!
Boys   It burns up homes and villages
     And miles of forest land.
Girls   If we are lax with fire,
     We've everything to lose;
All   It's up to us to keep it safe
     And wonderful to use.

SILLY MICE
(A Nonsense Poem)

Boys	There were four little mice
	Who lived in their hice;
Girls	Or was it four mouses
	Who lived in their houses?
Quartet	They sharpened their teeth
	On some telephone beeth;
Chorus	Well, perhaps they were booths
	Where they sharpened their tooths.
Boys	Then they rescued two gooses
	Caught up in some nooses;
Girls	Or it may have been neese
	That were strangling the geese.
Trio	When at last they were done
	With their work and their fun,
Chorus	The four little mice
	Hurried back to their hice.

SNOWMAN

Chorus	I made a chubby snowman
	Right out in my front yard;
Low V.	He had a hat and wooden broom
	So he could stand on guard.
Solo	I went to school and left him—
Chorus	When I returned toward night
	And took one look at Chubby,
	I knew there'd been a fight.
High V.	His body was much smaller,
	His broom was on the ground,
Chorus	And then I knew that Mr. Sun
	Had won the final round.

HALLOWEEN

Chorus	Oh, Halloween's the time of year
	We make believe we shake with fear
	To see a jack-o-lantern glow
	With bright red eyes at us below.
Solo 1	We quiver at the mad black cat,
Solo 2	The ghosts who roam, the wide-winged bat,
Solo 3	The owl that's hooting all around,
Solo 4	The misty goblins on the ground.
High V.	It's scary but we have such fun,
	And, when our outside tricks are done,
Low V.	We go back home and end the day
	The good old-fashioned ducking way.
Chorus	We never should be bad or mean
	But just have fun on Halloween.

LONG-AGO CHILDREN

Chorus   The children who lived in the long, long ago
Were all very different from us;
For instance, they walked many miles to their
    schools
While we ride in ease on the bus.

Girls   The mothers of long-ago boys and girls
Had to spin and weave their clothes;
We just go out and buy all we wear,

Chorus   From our heads right down to our toes.

Boys   Boys of the long-ago days were so brave;
When their fathers went hunting for game,
They took care of their mothers and guarded
    the homes—

Chorus   Would the boys of today do the same?

Girls   Long-ago girls learned to do many things;
While still very young, they could tell
When soap was made right or candles all done—

Chorus   Could the girls of today do as well?

Boys   The long-ago children bring shame to our
    hearts

Girls   Every time that we make such a fuss.

Chorus   We know we admire the things that *they* did,
But we wonder what they'd think of *us*!

WINKING EYES

Chorus	Last night before I went to sleep
	I looked up at the skies;
Quartet	I saw the moon, so round and full,
	The stars with winking eyes.
High V.	I lay back on my pillow
	And said a little prayer,
Low V.	To thank God for my golden friends
	Who winked and blinked up there.
Solo	And then *my* eyes began to blink;
Low V.	I rolled up in a heap.
High V.	The stars kept winking all night long
Chorus	While I was fast asleep.

JANUARY

Boys	If you like your weather cold,
All	January can't be beat.
Girls	Then the winter's setting in,
	Bringing snow and freezing sleet.
Boys	Get your ice skates, grab your sled,
	Race until your cheeks are red.
Quartet	Listen for the sleighbells' jingle—
	January's full of tingle.

NEW YEAR'S DAY

All	Happy New Year! Hear bells ring,
	Whistles blow and people sing.
Boys	Cheerful folks are everywhere,
	Resolutions fill the air.
Girls	Only good things we'll remember
	Of last year right through December.
All	We all welcome with good cheer
	This brand new and happy year!

VALENTINE

Girls I've sent a little valentine
       To someone that I love;
  All I drew a pretty heart on it
       And over that a dove.
Boys Right in the middle of the heart
       I printed, "I love you."
  All I know I'll get a valentine
       That says, "I love you, too."

GEORGE WASHINGTON

Chorus	George Washington was president
	Of our United States,
Solo 1	The first one that we ever had,
Chorus	And one of our first "greats."
Low V.	He started as a little boy
	By never telling lies,
High V.	By loving God so very much—
	Quite rare in one his size.
Solo 2	He did just what his parents asked
Solo 3	And showed respect toward all;
Low V.	He read a lot and was prepared
	To hear his country's call.
High V.	No wonder that a boy so fine
	Grew up to be so great—
Chorus	The "Father of our Country"
	We should try to imitate.

MADMEN

Boys	Many men are merry men
	But many men are mad;
All	Because they can't make money
	Every minute, they are sad.
Girls	Money means so much to them—
	As they amass more wealth,
	Their minds think only money,
All	And this affects their health.

AMERICAN EDUCATION WEEK

Girls	Every year on certain dates, Parents are invited To visit all our classrooms—
Chorus	My, we get excited!
Boys	We gather all our papers And put them in a book,
Chorus	Then hang up all our artwork And straighten out each nook.
Solo 1	We make them something special As a welcome to our class,
Solo 2	And tape it on the blackboard Or perhaps the windowglass.
Solo 3	This visit always shows our folks If we are doing well,
Chorus	And if we're not, then *watch out*, For they can always tell!

PRETTY PATTY

Boys	Pretty Patty Draper Made a picture on some paper
All	With paint and paste and purple-patterned plaid.
Girls	Her pa perused it proudly, Proclaimed his praises loudly,
All	And Pat was pretty proud to please her dad.

LINCOLN'S HAT

All	Lincoln was so very tall,
	His frame was slim and spare;
Solo 1	He didn't need to wear a hat
All	To prove that he was there.
Duet	But Lincoln wore a stovepipe hat
	That reached up to the sky;
Solo 2	He stood right out in every crowd,
All	His hat was up so high!

CIRCUS CLOWNS

High V.	Circus clowns will always tell you
	Life is a merry song.
Low V.	If you want to join the circus,
	They'll gladly take you along.
Solo 1	They have fun amusing children,
Solo 2	Making them laugh every day;
Chorus	They go everywhere,
	As their fun they share,
	For a clown's life is jolly and gay.
High V.	Circus clowns have funny faces,
	Painted right to a turn;
Low V.	They'd be glad to take you with them
	If some tricks you can learn.
Solo 3	They do juggling, they do tumbling,
	And walk wires, they say.
Chorus	They go everywhere,
	As their fun they share,
	For a clown's life is jolly and gay.

MARCH WINDS

Solo	March winds blow
	But I don't care,
Chorus	For signs of spring
	Are in the air.
Low V.	Now Mr. Winter
	Has to go,
Chorus	And with him all
	The ice and snow.
High V.	So come, March winds,
	Come blow and sing;
Chorus	We know you're here
	To bring the spring.

ST. PATRICK'S DAY

Solo 1	I love it on St. Patrick's Day
	When paper shamrocks bloom,
All	And we make other pretty things
	To decorate our room.
Boys	There's Mr. Big Potato Man
	With jolly, twinkling eyes
Girls	And dainty little golden harps,
	Not quite the proper size.
Solo 2	Sometimes we make an Irish hat,
Boys	The kind they wear to hunt;
Girls	It's high and wide with silken band,
	A buckle in the front.
Solo 3	And then to finish up just right
Boys	We make some pipes of clay,
All	And turn to shake each other's hands
	On good St. Patrick's Day.

MUSIC FAIRY

Chorus	Once there was a little boy
	Who didn't like to sing,
Trio	And when he went to music class
	He did the queerest thing.
High V.	When all the other children sang
	Their notes so sweet and high,
	He'd stick his fingers in his ears
Low V.	And start to moan and cry.
Solo 1	Perhaps before I tell you more
	About this little boy,
Med. V.	I should explain how fairies come
	To fill our lives with joy.
High V.	Each time a tiny child is born,
	Inside his little heart
	Is placed a music fairy
	With a very special art.
Chorus	This fairy makes you sing and hum
	And dance and march and jig,
	And, if you're very good to her,
	You'll keep her till you're big.
Solo 2	Now this queer boy just couldn't stand
	A soft artistic sound.
High V.	The fairy's crooked wand had turned
	His heartstrings all around.
Low V.	The music class was quite upset
	To hear his mournful moans,
	Each time their notes were high and sweet
	And beautiful their tones.
Med. V.	They called a music doctor
	Who did one simple thing—
Solo 3	He straightened out the fairy's wand,
Chorus	And now the boy can sing!
Trio	He loves to go to music class,
	His notes are clear and gay;
Chorus	The music fairy's happy too,
	She waves her wand all day.

MY GYMNASTIC DOLL *(Girls)*

All   My doll is gymnastic,
She's made out of plastic
And bends at the waist and the knees.

Solo 1   She's so energetic,
I feel sympathetic
Whenever she tries hard to please.

All   Her arms can go outward
Or twirl all aboutward—
She'll do any trick you suggest.

Solo 2   When we see her wiggling,
It makes us start giggling;

All   Of all my dolls she's the best.

Solo 3   She walks rather quickly
And never is sickly;
We know exercise keeps her well.

All   She's really fantastic,
My doll that's gymnastic;
I'm *so* proud of her, can't you tell?

EXCUSE ME

Chorus	When you pass in front of someone,
Boys	Always say, "Excuse me, please"
Girls	Or if you *must* interrupt,
Chorus	Say again, "Excuse me, please."

MOTHER'S DAY

All   Families are made up of fathers and of mothers,

Solo 1   And most of them we know have some sisters
     and some brothers.

Boys   But with all respect to Dad, whom we couldn't
     do without,

All   *Mom's* the one who makes the house a home,
     without a doubt.

Solo 2   It's Mother that we call for when we're sick or
     when we're hurt,

Solo 3   It's Mother that we ask to mend the tear in
     dress or shirt.

Girls   So let's not wait for Mother's Day to put
     on one big show—

All   Let every day be Mother's Day because we
     love her so.

FATHER'S DAY

Chorus   Fathers are wonderful people—

Solo 1   They go off to work every day

High V.   To earn enough money to help us
     Be happy at school and at play.

Low V.   We ask them for things that we've dreamed of,
     Or things that we've seen at the store,

Solo 2   And then when we have all we've asked for,

Chorus   We start right in asking for more.

Low V.   Now that their day is arriving,

High V.   We'll show them why they should be glad.

Chorus   Let's tell them how much we all love them,
     And let's take it easy on Dad.

MAYTIME

Girls	When the lilac's sweet perfume
	Fills the air and tulips bloom,
	It's Maytime, it's Maytime!
Boys	When the red of robin's breast
	Tells of birds' eggs in the nest,
	It's Maytime, it's Maytime!
Solo 1	When we see the leafy bough,
Solo 2	School is almost over now,
All	It's Maytime, it's Maytime!
Girls	Let us gather round and sing
	Of the nicest month in Spring,
All	It's Maytime, it's Maytime!

ARBOR DAY

Solo 1	It's Arbor Day!
Solo 2	Let's plant a tree,
All	A happy thing for all to see.
Girls	Trees are lovely
	To behold,
	No matter whether young or old.
Boys	So let's get smart
	And make a rule
	To plant a tree each year at school
All	On Arbor Day.

APRIL SHOWERS

Chorus	April's the month made for showers,
Girl	For soft gentle rain on your face,
High V.	For days bringing spring's happy promise
	Of jonquils' and daffodils' grace.
Chorus	The seeds in the ground get so thirsty,
	Then showers of April begin;
Low V.	They soften the soil and refresh it
	And help let the sunbeams creep in.
Girl	We're glad to have April's cool showers
Boy	That take all the frost from the earth,
Chorus	We're glad for the beautiful mornings,
	For spring and its yearly rebirth.

FLOWER FAIRIES

Girls   Flower fairies help us grow
         Our pretty flowers in a row,
Boys   Or in a circle, square, or star;
All   We call to them and there they are!
Boys   Children like to have them near
         Because the fairies bring them cheer.
Duet   These flower fairies work so hard
         To beautify each lawn and yard;
Girls   They tint the flowers with good taste,
         Not one small minute do they waste.
All   And when their work is done, they play
         And dance the rest of the night and day.

MY TREE

Chorus	The tree I love so dearly Grows near a little lane,
High V.	The one I take to go to school And come back home again.
Low V.	The other trees that grow there Are very lovely too, But this one seems most friendly, A haven, safe and true.
Trio	One day when I was running To get to school on time, I fell and bruised my elbow Right near this friend of mine.
High V.	The tree looked down serenely And seemed to whisper low,
Solo 1	"Don't cry for such a little thing, It isn't much, you know!"
Chorus	And as I sat beneath its limbs On moss so soft and cool,
Low V.	The pain all seemed to go away And off I rushed to school.
Solo 2	You'll never feel alone and sad But happy as can be,
Chorus	If you can find a steadfast friend, A true friend like my tree.

HAPPY SUMMER

High V.	"Have a happy summer!"
Chorus	What a funny thing to say!
	For summer's always happy
	And summer's alway gay.
Med. V.	This is true with most folks
	When working or at play,
Low V.	As long as they do everything
	The safe, wise way.
Chorus	Let's all do things this summer
	The safe, wise way!
High V.	Don't bake in the sun too long,
	You're not a cake, you know;
Low V.	Take a buddy friend with you
	Most places that you go—
Chorus	Especially when swimming
	Or on a woodland hike,
Med. V.	But don't expect to ride him
	Double on your bike.
Chorus	Let's all do things this summer
	The safe, wise way!
Med. V.	Ease up on your playing,
	Help Mom and Daddy too,
Low V.	Bathe a bit more often
	And sleep the whole night through.
Chorus	Have a happy summer,
	Think "safety" every day;
High V.	Be wise and safe all summer,
	Safe and wise and gay.
Chorus	Let's all do things this summer
	The safe, wise way!

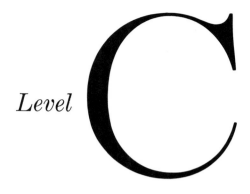

Level C

OLD SWIMMIN' HOLE

Boys When Grandpa was quite little,
His one and only goal,
As soon as school was ended,
Was the good old swimmin' hole.

Girls This was a bit of water,
Secluded, crystal-clear,
Where boys could swim for hours
With a minimum of fear.

Quartet 1 From all that Grandpa tells us,
They jumped from limbs of trees

Quartet 2 Or swung from lengthy cables
Like the man on the trapeze.

All Last week when I was swimming
In our brand new swimming pool,
Grandpa came to visit
And decided to keep cool

Girls By putting on his swim trunks
And diving in with me.

Boys He said, "This beats the swimmin' hole
Or swinging from a tree."

All But I can't help regretting,
As I dive and jump and roll,
That I didn't live in Grandpa's time
To enjoy his swimmin' hole.

FISHING IN THE LAKE

Girls   Fisherman, fisherman, out in your boat,
          How do you feel when the waves make you float?
Boys   I feel like a captain, guiding my ship,
          Surveying the ocean as waves rise and dip.
Girls   Fisherman, fisherman, throw out your line,
          So you'll have some fish when you're ready to
             dine.
Boys   I'm watching and waiting and eager to reel;
          Oh, I've got a nibble—it should make a meal.
Girls   Fisherman, fisherman, lucky at last,
          Don't rock the boat as you pull it in fast.
Boys   Steady, now, steady, it seems to be strong
          But it will be mine before very long.
Girls   Fisherman, fisherman, how did you do?
Boys   Shucks, all I caught was a muddy old shoe!

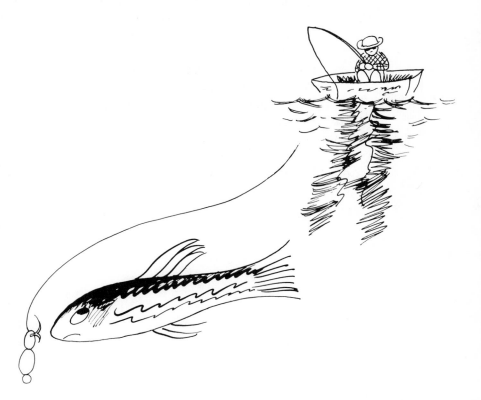

BIG WORDS

All	Some words we use are very small
	So that we doubt their use at all.
	But there are those we need so much—
	The A's and I's and O's and such.
Girls	Then we grow bigger and we find
	Much bigger words come to our mind;
Boys	In order to express a thought,
	Those smaller words would count for naught.
Trio 1	To better our vocabulary
	We rush to any dictionary
All	And see words that are beneficial,
	Good clear words, not prejudicial.
Girls	We seem to have no more compunction,
	Seeking words with special function;
Boys	Using them is not horrendous
	When our list becomes tremendous.
Trio 2	Rather, it soon seems hilarious
	As we grow much more gregarious
All	And increase our risibility,
	For we have this great facility
	To get chummy and loquacious,
	Even makes us feel flirtatious.
Girls	Better call a moratorium
Boys	Before we rate a sanitorium—
Solo	This has all been said in jest;
All	Maybe simpler words are best!

MUSIC

Girls	When children think of music,
	They think of happy notes
All	That bubble out of girls and boys,
	A sound that wafts and floats.
Solo 1	Or they remember lullabies—
All	All mothers know a few
	To sing when Baby's overwrought
	And nothing else will do.
Boys	But there are other kinds of songs
	To make life more worthwhile:
Girls	The sad ones in a minor key
	Would never make you smile,
Trio	But they can make you quiet
	And pensive and apart,
All	If people are sincere enough
	To sing them from the heart.
Boys	Then there is marching music
	That makes us tap our feet,
Girls	And family get-togethers
	Where loving voices meet.
Solo 2	At times we sit and listen
	To a symphony or two,
All	For to be real music lovers
	We must hear all kinds, it's true.
Solo 3	Even animals like music—
Boys	Many farmers tell the yarn
	That their cows will give more milk
	When there's music in the barn.
Girls	There are many kinds of music,
	But the songs I like to hear
	Are the lovely Christmas carols—
All	They're repeated every year.
Boys	Oh, everyone loves music
	From birth to ninety-five,
	For music makes us happy,
All	Happy just to be alive.

MOON FLIGHT

All   In the days before men
       Like Schirra and John Glenn,
       We thought of the moon quite a lot.

Boys   Would we fly there in ease
       To a moon made of cheese?
       Would the surface be cold or too hot?

Girls   How about the old rhyme
       Of the cow in her prime,
       The one that jumped over the moon?

All   Would we hit her some night
       If we met her in flight,
       Having fun with the dish and the spoon?
          (pause)

Boys   Well, we don't have to dream
       Any more, it would seem,
       Since the astronauts gave us the facts.

Girls   They have found it to be
       Very different, you see,
       For there's many a thing the moon lacks.

Solo 1   Of plants it is bare,
Solo 2   There's less gravity there.
Solo 3   No water, no air, no known life;

Boys   With its craters and such
       It would not offer much
       For a man to fly up with his wife.

Girl   So until I get big,
       I'll learn all I can dig
       From the books on our library shelf,

All   But let it be known
       That, when I'm fully grown,
       I want to find out for myself.

SALAMANDER

All	Susie spied a salamander
	Saunt'ring down the street.
Girls	"What a silly sight!" she whispered;
	"Still, he's sort of sweet."
Boys	So she snatched the salamander,
	Stuffed him in her blouse,
	Kept him safe and soft and snuggly
	Till she reached her house.
Duet 1	Now she feeds the salamander,
Duet 2	Likes to watch him grow,
All	Strokes his stripes while he is swimming
	'Cause she loves him so.

RAINY DAYS

Solo 1	Our first thought on a rainy day is,
All	"Gosh, what can I do?"
Boys	For outdoor play is off our list,
	Our swim and boating too.
Girls	But rainy days can be a gift
	To all of us, you know,
All	If we can make our spirits rise
	To high instead of low.
Solo 2	For we can dash some letters off,
Solo 3	Draw pictures just for fun,
Solo 4	Or help our mom to bake a cake—
All	This pleases everyone.
Boys	Or we could meditate awhile
	On what life's all about,
Girls	On how to love each other—
	This would do us good, no doubt.
Quartet	But we don't need to stay indoors
	Because some rain must fall;
All	We don our rainy weather clothes,
	Umbrella, boots, and all.
Boys	And then we go out visiting
Girls	A friend or, maybe, two.
All	We know much-needed rain is good;
	The sun will soon shine through.

LITTLE MAN IN A TREE

Girls   I don't believe in fairies
          And I don't believe in elves,
All   And I never thought that leprechauns
          Did magic by themselves.
Boys   But something funny happened
          When I was rather small,
          One day when I went out to play
          With Puppy and my ball.
Girls   As soon as we were tired,
          We rested 'neath a tree
          And then I heard a crackly voice
          Calling down to me.
Boys   I knew the dog had heard it
          'Cause his ears began to rise
          And he was sort of puzzled
          As he opened wide his eyes.
All   I glanced into the branches
          Of the tree above my head
          And spied a little wizened man
          In funny pants of red.
Girls   He wore a tiny green coat
          With tails that hung down long,
          And waved a silver hammer
          As he sang a merry song.
Trio 1   My eyes closed for a minute;
Trio 2   Once more we heard his call.
Boys   But when I looked above again
          He wasn't there at all.
Girls   So I don't believe in fairies
          And I don't believe in elves,
All   But I wonder now if leprechauns
          Do magic by themselves.

MARY PAT

Chorus	Mary Pat's a darling And she's a perfect dear. But Mary Pat does odd things That fill our hearts with fear.
High V.	She hears a kitten crying, It's caught up in a tree,
Chorus	And she must climb up after it To bring it down, you see.
Low V.	She sees a big boy fighting With someone small and frail; Then she steps in to break it up And gets hurt, without fail.
Solo	Or when she spies a swimmer Flound'ring on the lake,
Chorus	She yells for help, then dives right in— What a lifeguard she would make!
High V.	So Mary Pat's a darling, Her goodness runs so deep,
Chorus	But she must learn to look a bit Before she starts to leap.

MR. MOON

All	Whenever I look at the sky at night
	And see the moon with its golden light,
Duet	I spy a face as plain as can be—
All	It's Mr. Moon looking down at me.
Girls	I stare and wonder what he must think,
	As he glows so bright and the stars all wink;
Solo 1	This crazy earth seems blithe and free
All	And Mr. Moon's glancing down at me.
Boys	Then I recall, as I watch and stare,
	The astronauts were away up there.
Solo 2	It seems to be such a mystery
All	As Mr. Moon keeps his eye on me.
Girls	I hope some day, after I've been taught
Boys	All I need to know for an astronaut,
Solo 3	That *I'll* shoot up and land there too;
All	Then with Mr. Moon I'll look down on *you*.

A PARADE

Girls	Come, watch the soldiers marching by,
	Their feet in rhythm, heads held high,
Quartet 1	And how our flag waves merrily,
	Its beauty there for all to see.
All	My eyes get bright, my heart beats fast,
	Whenever a parade goes past.
Boys	Oh, hear the fifers as they come,
	The drummer boy who beats the drum,
Quartet 2	The leader man with gusty shout,
	And shiny trumpets blasting out.
All	My eyes get bright, my heart beats fast,
	Whenever a parade goes past.
Girls	Just see the majorettes who prance,
	Their knees up high in marching dance,
	Batons that glitter, twist, and twirl
	As signals pass from girl to girl.
All	My eyes get bright, my heart beats fast,
	Whenever a parade goes past.
Boys	It's great to watch a good parade—
	I listen till the shrill notes fade,
	And when it's gone too far to see
	I keep it in my memory.
All	My eyes get bright, my heart beats fast,
	Whenever a parade goes past.

SLEEPYHEAD

Girls	"Wake up, wake up!" my mother said;
	"It's time that you were out of bed."
Trio	I moaned and mumbled in my sleep,
Boys	Then rolled myself into a heap.
Girls	"Wake up, wake up!" my mother cried,
	Or you will miss your schoolbus ride."
Trio	I told myself that sleep was done
Boys	And stretched my toes out, one by one.
All	"Wake up!" I heard my mother call,
Boys	As slowly I walked down the hall.
Trio	I ran into the bathroom door
	And closed my eyes in sleep once more.
Boys	"Wake up, get up!" My father's voice
	Was roaring mad and left no choice.
All	So . . . (*pause*)
Girls	I dressed myself and washed my face,
Boys	Ran down the stairs, sat at my place;
Trio	I ate some food, slipped off my chair,
Girls	Raced out the door, my bus was there.
Boys	Was in my class with time galore!
	(*pause*)
All	Now *what* was all the shouting for?

(Have children draw out the word,
SO-O-O-O, then pause. The next five lines
should start out at a moderate rate of speed,
then gain momentum till the climax,
"With time galore!" After a pause,
have the last line said slowly by all.)

SHARING TIME

Boys	Most days when I get home from school,
	My mother's waiting there—
Girls	She lets me tell about my day,
	My "how" and "when" and "where."
Boy 1	I have a snack, some fruit and milk,
Girl 1	She has a cup of tea;
All	We do enjoy this special time
	Of camaraderie.
Girl 2	And then she goes about her work
Boy 2	And I change clothes for play.
All	We're both a little better
	For our sharing time each day.

CLOCKS

All   The clock on the steeple is handsome and grand;
It makes our town hall seem the best in the
      land.

Boys   Whenever the half or the hour comes round,
Its ding-dong rings out with a far-reaching
      sound.

Trio 1   How different the clock on our living room wall!
Its face doesn't have any numbers at all.

Girls   You have to be clever to figure the time,

All   Though sometimes you're helped by its musical
      chime.

Trio 2   You surely have seen little traveling clocks;
When closed up they look like a small leather
      box.

Boys   Some of them tell what the temperature is—
My dad on a business trip always takes his.

All   What would we do without clocks in our home?

Solo 1   The alarm in the bedroom all outlined in chrome,

Girls   The kitchen clock shaped like a teapot of blue,

Boys   The dining room clock where a bird says,
      "cuckoo!"

All   Electric, magnetic and wind-ups with springs,
Pendulum, grandfather, all sorts of things.

Solo 2   Surely we know from their ticks and their tocks

All   That life would be dull if we didn't have clocks.

FEBRUARY

All	February's very short,
	The shortest month of all;
Duet 1	Its days are only twenty-eight,
	Except when leap years fall.
All	Then February twenty-ninth
	Gives us an extra day
	For riding down the hill on sleds
	Or using horse and sleigh.
Boys	This month has double holidays,
	For two great men were born:
Solo 1	George on the twenty-second day,
Solo 2	Abe on the twelfth day's morn.
Girls	It's on the fourteenth lovers send
	Each other valentines,
	With hearts and arrows well drawn in
	And love in all the lines.
Duet 2	February's very short
	But we find time and ways
All	To make our decorations
	For all its special days.

COLLECTIONS

Quartet 1	It's really common knowledge
	(And a boon to everyone)
All	That we have certain hobbies
	We can work at just for fun.
Girls	Most popular, we've noticed,
	Is collecting special things—
Boys	It's done by young and old alike,
	By poor men and by kings.
All	There are stamp and coin collections,
	And matchbook covers too,
	Teapots, pitchers, baseball cards,
	To mention just a few.
Girls	Some folks save dolls or angels,
	Ceramic pastel birds,
Quartet 2	And some have rocks or butterflies,
	Too beautiful for words.
All	Then there are first editions,
	And paintings by great men,
	Jade jewelry and porcelain,
Solo	Old swords from "way back when."
Quartet 3	A music box collection
	Will any home enhance;
Boys	You wind them up and listen
	And watch the figures dance.
Girls	So no matter what you've chosen
	To collect and show with pride,
All	The main thing is the sense of joy
	Collectors feel inside.

ABRAHAM LINCOLN

Chorus	Many, many years have passed
	Since Lincoln lived upon this earth,
High V.	But while he lived he proved to all
	His goodness and his sterling worth.
Solo 1	Some liked to call him "Honest Abe";
	His speeches were so full of truth.
Low V.	He often prayed to God for help,
	This tall and slender, dark-haired youth.
Solo 2	Hard work was never hard for him;
Solo 3	He hadn't much of this world's goods,
Chorus	And so he helped his folks to build
	A small log cabin in the woods.
Low V.	It hurt him very much to learn
	That people still made slaves of men
High V.	And women too, and so he fought
	Until they all were free again.
Solo 4	So let's salute our Abraham,
	A poor man made a president;
Chorus	He helped our country's history
	By showing what its freedom meant.

MAKE SOMEONE HAPPY

Solo 1	Did you make someone happy today?
All	Did you make someone sad feel gay?
Boys	If you haven't been trying,
	Someone may be crying
	Because his blue sky turned to gray.
All	Just stop for a minute and say,
	"Did I make someone happy today?"
Solo 2	There are so many ways that you might
All	Make the day for somebody more bright.
Girls	You can give help to Mother,
	Dad, sister, or brother.
	This will make your own troubles seem light.
All	Just stop for a minute and say,
	"Did I make someone happy today?"
Solo 3	You can help as the day goes along
All	By *not* doing something that's wrong.
Boys	Why not give up dumb fighting
	Or screaming or biting
	And show that you've learned to be strong?
All	Just stop for a minute and say,
	"Did I make someone happy today?"
Solo 4	No matter which method you choose,
All	Try hard to be kind—you can't lose!
Girls	You'll feel merry and glowing
	Just simply by knowing
	You've helped brush away someone's blues.
All	Just stop for a minute and say,
	"Did I make someone happy today?"

NATURE'S COLORS

All	Blue is the sky on a bright, cheery day,
	Green grows the grass in the new month of May.
Girls	Mountains glow purple at sunset time,
	Deep rosy pink if you let your eyes climb.
Boys	Apples are red on the old crooked tree,
	Much darker red are the cherries we see.
Duet 1	Oranges bright give the color its name,
All	And, of course, tangerines are colored the same.
Girls	Cows in the meadow are brownish in hue,
Trio 1	Their eyes, too, are brown as they look up at you.
All	The barn, newly painted, is lovely and red;
	Inside, golden straw makes each animal's bed.
Girls	Buttercups yellow abound in the field;
	Peaches stay peach even when they are peeled.
Boys	Deep ocean water, its surface of green
	With blue all mixed in, makes a beautiful scene.
Duet 2	Flowers of violet, lemon, and cream,
Trio 2	Royal blue and rose red, all part of the dream.
All	Nature's enchanting, bewitching and free,
	There for our pleasure, for you and for me.

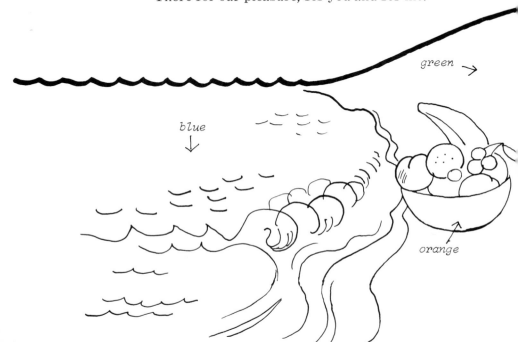

A PICTURE

Boys	I looked out my window and what did I see?
All	A picture unfolding itself just for me;
Quartet 1	The outline of three baby deer on a hill,
Solo 1	A large, jaunty robin with bright yellow bill,
Solo 2	Some sheep in the meadow, starting to graze,
Quartet 2	And there in the distance a light morning haze.
All	An artist could paint this to bring himself fame,
	And here it was mine through my large window frame.

OUT IN THE COUNTRY

Solo	It's wonderful out in the country,
	Where we live the whole year round,
Chorus	In spring when the earth starts its giving
	And new life shoots up through the ground.
High V.	Each day finds the grass growing greener,
	The trees bearing blossoms in May;
Low V.	Yet, as nature grows heavy with goodness,
	Our hearts seem to grow light and gay.
Solo	Then just when we're used to the springtime,
	Summer starts weaving its spell,
Chorus	Its glorious days filled with sunlight
	To make people happy and well.
High V.	But before very long we have autumn
	With colors quite lovely to see;
Low V.	That's harvesting time for the farmer
	And back-to-school time for me.
Chorus	Then winter with snow-covered meadows
	Brings out all the iceboats and sleds;
Low V.	You can bet when the cold day over
	We are glad to be tucked in our beds.
High V.	Yes, it's wonderful out in the country,
	Summer, winter, the springtime or fall,
Chorus	For we have what so many are missing—
	Life and health and the baby bird's call.

OCEAN

Chorus	Ocean so beautiful, ocean so blue,
	I was glad yesterday, gazing at you.
High V.	Waves rolled in gently, breezes were light,
	Calm weather made you a beautiful sight!
Chorus	Ocean so mighty, today you are green;
	What made you change to a monster so mean?
Low V.	Waves churn in anger, winds shriek at me,
	Clouds hide the sunshine; you're fearful to see.
Chorus	Ocean so beautiful, treat me with care
High V.	When winds are gentle, when days are fair.
Low V.	But if you frown with an ominous air,
Chorus	Churning and turning, then I'll beware!

SNOWFLAKES

Girls	Snowflakes falling from the sky,
	What a pretty sight you make!
All	Soft and shiny, silv'ry white,
	Piling tiny flake on flake.
Boys	When you cover hills and trees,
	It's a painting that's so grand;
All	Nothing seems quite real to me
	And all the world's a fairyland!

IN THE DENTIST'S OFFICE

All	Waiting in the dentist's office
	Can be lots of fun,
	If you just sit back and try
	To study everyone.
High V.	There's the cute but tired mother
	With two little boys;
Duet 1	They won't let her rest a minute,
	Fighting over toys.
Low V.	One Mom with a worried smile
	Tries to keep her "cool,"
Duet 2	Looking at the cracked front tooth
	Sonny got at school.
All	The waiting-room is filled with people,
	Children, big and small,
Low V.	And *one* man who anxiously
	Awaits the dentist's call.
High V.	Then the inner door is opened
	And I hear my name—
All	Waiting time is nothing
	When I play this waiting game.

CRAZY COOTS

All   Coots are on the lake,
High V.   So my mother called out, "Look!
Here are those crazy water birds
I showed you in a book."
Low V.   They were floating on the lake
And as busy as could be,
Dipping down for water plants
That we could hardly see.
Solo 1   Bills were small and yellow,
Solo 2   Little tails were on their rear,
All   And they turned their bodies over
So they seemed to disappear.
High V.   Then a couple up on land
Waddled nonchalantly past
And we got a perfect look,
All   'Cause they couldn't waddle fast.
Low V.   Wings and tails were short,
Voices made a raucous sound;
Duet   Toes had membrane flaps
That helped them swim around.
High V.   Mom said, "Crazy as a coot?
Not these water birds we've seen;
All   They may look it but they're not,
As they keep our water clean."

ANIMAL DOCTOR

Girls   I have a very special friend,
          The best I've ever met;
All   He's called a veterinarian
          Or often just "the vet."
Solo 1   He's helped me with my animals
          More times than I can tell;
Solo 2   With shots and operations
          He has kept my loved pets well.
Boys   I listen to the stories
          Of the cattle he has healed,
Trio   The poor cow who was giving birth
          To her calf out in the field,
Boys   The chickens and the pigs and sows
          He must inoculate,
Girls   The sick dogs that were brought to him,
          How they recuperate.
Boys   I love my animal doctor;
Girls   He's big and strong, you see,
All   But gentle with my animals
          And a real good friend to me.

GULLS

All	Gulls are fascinating birds—
	I love to watch them fly.
High V.	They soar and dip so gracefully,
	Then rise into the sky.
All	They always look so clean and neat,
	Not colorful and bright,
High V.	But when they're flying near the sea,
	Oh, what a lovely sight!
Solo	Their eyesight must be very keen,
Low V.	For they have but to stare
	From way up high, then zoom straight down
	To catch fish unaware.
High V.	Now gulls make such a different sound,
	A softened kind of screech;
All	Just listen to their chattering
	Next time you're at the beach.
Low V.	And you may see one watch his feet
	While resting after meals;
All	Nobody knows just why he does
	Or how he thinks or feels.
High V.	Yes, gulls are fascinating birds
	And, if I had my way,
All	I'd live right at the ocean's edge
	And study them all day.

OUR WORLD

All	The world is full of beauty,
	Of kindness, joy, and love,
Boys	Of soft green grass to walk on,
	The azure sky above,
Girls	Of birds that sing and warble,
Duet	Fresh air and endless sea,
Girls	All there to make us happy,
	All there for you and me.
Boys	But now this earthly heaven
	Is threatened by a foe,
Girls	As once there came a serpent
	To Eden years ago.
Solo 1	Some streams have been polluted,
Solo 2	Our fish supply won't last;
All	We can't go swimming safely
	As we used to in the past.
Boys	And what of land abuses,
	Removing helpful trees
	But not replacing them?
All	Is there no hope for these?
Girls	Our cities and our townships
	That used to have just fog
Boys	Are going downhill quickly
	With their poison-laden smog.
Girls	Now MAN has caused these problems,
All	So MAN (that's me and you!)
Boys	Can give us back our clean land,
All	Clean air and water too.

BOOKS

High V.	Are you ever lonesome
	On a rainy, rainy day?
Low V.	Do you wonder what to do
	When rain keeps friends away?
Chorus	Reach out for a good book,
	The best friend you can find;
Med. V.	It's sure to make you happy
	If you read the proper kind.
Duet 1	You can go on a long trip
	To India or France;
Duet 2	You can learn how to cook
	Or to do the latest dance.
Med. V.	Some books are so funny
	You have to laugh out loud,
Chorus	Some books tell of heroes
	Who made their country proud.
High V.	Take care of these book friends,
Low V.	Respect them, old or new,
Chorus	And you will find them true friends,
	Always helping you.

TRAIN WHISTLE *(Boys)*

Light V.	What a wonderful sound is the steam train whistle
	As the train flies through the night.
Heavy V.	It's hearty and friendly and comfort-giving
	After Mom's turned out the light.
Chorus	I lie in the dark with both ears open
	And hear every quiet sound:
	The chirp of the cricket, the katydids,
	The deep-throated bark of the hound.
Solo 1	Then the quiet is shattered by one shrill whistle,
Solo 2	Another that's long and mellow—
Chorus	The steam train is hurrying home through the night,
	What a magical sound to a fellow!
Light V.	After it's vanished, I close eyes and ears,
	With a feeling of peace heave a sigh.
Heavy V.	A nice dreamy feeling comes over me then,
	Hypnotized by my steam lullaby.
Quartet	It seems that my mom would prefer diesel trains
	That keep our clean air free from dust,
Chorus	But give me a steam train with all of its noise
	And a whistle I know I can trust.

KEEP TRYING

All	Be honest! *(pause)*
Girls	Make integrity your aim,
Boys	Truth and fairness try to claim,
All	Don't sell out for wealth or fame.
Solo 1	Be trustworthy! *(pause)*
All	So your neighbor can depend
	On your actions as a friend,
Quartet	From beginning to the end.
All	Be diligent! *(pause)*
Trio 1	Use each minute of the day,
Trio 2	Whether working or at play,
All	In a good and useful way.
Solo 2	Be pleasant! *(pause)*
Girls	Smile with ease when life's a song;
All	Try to smile when things go wrong,
Boys	Make your sense of humor strong.
All	Be kind! *(pause)*
Boys	Share with those who are in need,
	Help a slower child to read,
Girls	Show your love in every deed.
All	Earth would be a finer place
	If we'd show our better face.

RAIN

Boys	"Oh, it's raining again," said Tommy,
Boy 1	As he opened the kitchen door;
Boys	"I thought it had rained so much all week
	That it never would rain any more."
Girls	"But we need lots of rain," said Mother,
	"If we want pretty flowers, you know;
Girl 1	And the earth needs this moisture to water our farm
Girls	And to make all our vegetables grow."
Boys	"I suppose that is true," said Tommy,
	"But this seems more than moisture to me;
Boy 2	For I'm sure that most plants get along on much less
Boys	And *this* rainfall would grow a big tree."
Girls	"Stop grumbling all day, please, Tommy,"
Girl 2	Begged Mother, impatient at last;
Girls	"Don't you know that we need all this rain for our wells
	And without it we'd thirst pretty fast?"
Boys	"No, I never knew that," said Tommy,
	"But you've certainly made it quite plain;
All	So now that I know how important it is,
	I'll try to be grateful for rain."

GOOD MORNING

Girls Good morning! Those are loving words
When I wake up each day
To hear my mother's cheery voice,
A voice both kind and gay.

Boys Good morning! makes my life secure
When I come down to eat
And hear my father's hearty voice,
At breakfast when we meet.

Quartet 1 Good morning! Those are pleasant words
When I arrive at school

All To have my teacher welcome me,
My friends too, as a rule.

Boys Good morning! Who'd begrudge us that,
Girls What decent person could?
Quartet 2 For those two words have magic sounds
That make each morning good.

HOME

Solo 1	I've heard it said by certain folks,
High V.	(And said quite merrily,)
Chorus	"Oh, any place I hang my hat
	Is home, sweet home to me!"
High V.	But I can't seem to feel that way;
	My home is set apart,
Low V.	For when I hang my hat up there
	I also hang my heart.
Duet 1	Home means to me a house of love
	Where God's name starts the day,
High V.	Where tears are dried and quarrels patched
	And hurts are kissed away.
Solo 2	It means my mother's smile so dear,
	Her frown when we are bad,
Low V.	My father's voice when evening comes,
	An evening gay and glad,
Chorus	The family gathered at a feast,
	All spirits running high,
Duet 2	An hour round the fireplace
	With stories bye and bye.
Solo 3	The goodness of companionship,
Solo 4	The harmony of song,
Chorus	That's how I feel about my home,
	A place where I belong.